Girliness
is next to
Godliness

A PROMISE JOURNAL

...inspired by life

Girliness Is Next to Godliness
© 2008 Ellie Claire, Inc.
www.ellieclaire.com

Compiled by Barbara Farmer
Designed by Naomi Solum

Scripture references are from the following sources: The Holy Bible, New International Version® NIV®. © 1973, 1978, 1984 by International Bible Society. Used by permission of Zondervan. The New King James Version (NKJV). Copyright © 1982 by Thomas Nelson, Inc. Used by permission. The Message. © 1993, 1994, 1995, 1996, 2000, 2001, 2002 by Eugene Peterson. Used by permission of NavPress, Colorado Springs, CO. The New Revised Standard Version (NRSV) of the Bible, © 1989. Division of Christian Education, National Council of Churches. Used by permission of Zondervan Publishing House, Licensee. The Holy Bible, New Living Translation (NLT) copyright © 1996 by permission of Tyndale House Publishers, Inc., Wheaton, IL. www.newlivingtranslation.com. The New Century Version® (NCV). Copyright © 1987, 1988, 1991 by Thomas Nelson, Inc. Used by permission. The NEW AMERICAN STANDARD BIBLE ® (NASB), Copyright © The Lockman Foundation 1960, 1962, 1963, 1968, 1971, 1972, 1973, 1975, 1977, 1995. Used by permission. (www.Lockman.org). All rights reserved.

Excluding Scripture verses, references to men and masculine pronouns have been replaced with gender-neutral references.

ISBN 978-1-934770-02-3
Printed in China

Girliness

is next to

Godliness

A PROMISE JOURNAL

Free to Be You

There's a special kind of freedom women enjoy: freedom to share innermost thoughts, to ask a favor, to show their true feelings. The freedom simply to be themselves.

> Dance like there's nobody watching
> Love like you'll never get hurt
> Sing like there's nobody listening
> Live like it's heaven on earth
> And speak from the heart to be heard.
>
> WILLIAM W. PURKEY

Be content with who you are, and don't put on airs. God's strong hand is on you; He'll promote you at the right time. Live carefree before God; He is most careful with you.

1 PETER 5:6-7 THE MESSAGE

Girliness is next to Godliness

*Happiness comes of the capacity to feel deeply, to enjoy simply,
to think freely, to risk life, to be needed.*
STORM JAMESON

Simple Things

I still find each day too short for all the thoughts I want to think, all the walks I want to take, all the books I want to read, and all the friends I want to see. The longer I live, the more my mind dwells upon the beauty and the wonder of the world.

JOHN BURROUGHS

God is the One who gives seed to the farmer and bread for food. He will give you all the seed you need and make it grow so there will be a great harvest from your goodness. He will make you rich in every way so that you can always give freely. And your giving through us will cause many to give thanks to God. This service you do not only helps the needs of God's people, it also brings many more thanks to God.

2 CORINTHIANS 9:10-12 NCV

Girliness is next to Godliness

Grant me the power of saying things too simple and too sweet for words.
COVENTRY PATMORE

_____

_____

_____

_____

_____

_____

_____

_____

_____

_____

God Loves You

Just as there comes a warm sunbeam into every cottage window, so comes a love-beam of God's care for every separate need.

NATHANIEL HAWTHORNE

It is clear to us, friends, that God not only loves you very much but also has put His hand on you for something special.

1 THESSALONIANS 1:4 THE MESSAGE

Listening to God is a firsthand experience.... God invites you to vacation in His splendor. He invites you to feel the touch of His hand. He invited you to feast at His table. He wants to spend time with you.

MAX LUCADO

Girliness is next to Godliness

Open your hearts to the love God instills.... God loves you tenderly. What He gives you is not to be kept under lock and key, but to be shared.

MOTHER TERESA

_____

_____

_____

_____

_____

_____

_____

_____

_____

_____

Food, Fashion, and Fun!

I base my fashion taste on what doesn't itch.

GILDA RADNER

Fashion is something that goes in one year and out the other.

Why do you spend your money on junk food, your hard-earned cash on cotton candy? Listen to Me, listen well: Eat only the best, fill yourself with only the finest. Pay attention, come close now, listen carefully to My life-giving, life-nourishing words.

ISAIAH 55:2-3 THE MESSAGE

We are indeed much more than what we eat, but what we eat can nevertheless help us to be much more than what we are.

ADELLE DAVIS

Girliness is next to Godliness

There are four basic food groups, milk chocolate, dark chocolate, white chocolate, and chocolate truffles.

Lovely Days

Our Creator would never have made such lovely days and given us the deep hearts to enjoy them, above and beyond all thought, unless we were meant to be immortal.

NATHANIEL HAWTHORNE

How precious to me are Your thoughts, O God!
How vast is the sum of them!
Were I to count them,
they would outnumber the grains of sand.
When I awake,
I am still with You.

PSALM 139:17-18 NIV

The innocent brightness of a new born day is lovely yet.

WILLIAM WORDSWORTH

Girliness is next to Godliness

Instead of a gem, or even a flower, we should cast the gift of a lovely thought into the heart of a friend, that would be giving as the angels give.
George MacDonald

_____

_____

_____

_____

_____

_____

_____

_____

_____

_____

Girliness is next to Godliness

Sister to Sister

We were a strange little band of characters, trudging through life
sharing diseases and toothpaste, coveting one another's desserts,
hiding shampoo, borrowing money, locking each other out of our
rooms, inflicting pain and kissing to heal it in the same instant,
loving, laughing, defending, and trying to figure out the common
thread that bound us all together.

ERMA BOMBECK

Everybody can be great. Because anybody can serve. You don't
have to have a college degree to serve. You don't have to make your
subject and your verb agree to serve.... You only need a heart full of
grace. A soul generated by love.

MARTIN LUTHER KING JR.

Girliness is next to Godliness

Sisters, we taught you how to live in a way that will please God, and you are living that way. Now we ask and encourage you in the Lord Jesus to live that way even more.

1 THESSALONIANS 4:1 NCV

A Heart Full of Grace

Have you ever thought that in every action of grace in your heart you have the whole omnipotence of God engaged to bless you?

ANDREW MURRAY

We throw open our doors to God and discover at the same moment that He has already thrown open His door to us. We find ourselves standing where we always hoped we might stand—out in the wide open spaces of God's grace and glory, standing tall and shouting our praise.

ROMANS 5:2 THE MESSAGE

Look deep within yourself and recognize what brings life and grace into your heart. It is this that can be shared with those around you. You are loved by God. This is an inspiration to love.

CHRISTOPHER DE VINCK

Girliness is next to Godliness

There is no rest in the heart of God until He knows that we are at rest in His grace.
LLOYD JOHN OGILVIE

Encouragement Is Awesome

Oh, the comfort, the inexpressible comfort of feeling safe with a person—having neither to weigh thoughts nor measure words, but pouring them all right out just as they are, chaff and grain together, certain that a faithful hand will take and sift them, keep what is worth keeping and then, with the breath of kindness, blow the rest away.

DINAH MARIA MULOCK CRAIK

Encourage one another daily, as long as it is called Today.

HEBREWS 3:13 NIV

Some days, it is enough encouragement just to watch the clouds break up and disappear, leaving behind a blue patch of sky and bright sunshine that is so warm upon my face. It's a glimpse of divinity; a kiss from heaven.

Girliness is next to Godliness

Encouragement is awesome. It has the capacity to...actually change the course of another human being's day, week, or life.
CHARLES R. SWINDOLL

_____

_____

_____

_____

_____

_____

_____

_____

_____

_____

Girliness is next to Godliness

The Gift of Miracles

There are only two ways to live your life. One is as though nothing is a miracle. The other is as though everything is a miracle.

RICHARD CRASHAW

Because of His great love for us, God, who is rich in mercy, made us alive with Christ even when we were dead in transgressions.... And God raised us up with Christ and seated us with Him in the heavenly realms in Christ Jesus, in order that in the coming ages He might show the incomparable riches of His grace, expressed in His kindness to us in Christ Jesus.

EPHESIANS 2:4-7 NIV

Girliness is next to Godliness

I think miracles exist in part as gifts and in part as clues
that there is something beyond the flat world we see.
PEGGY NOONAN

Our Hearts Entwined

May the Lord direct your hearts into the love of God and into the
steadfastness of Christ.

2 THESSALONIANS 3:4-5 NASB

The fullness of our heart is expressed in our eyes, in our touch, in
what we write, in what we say, in the way we walk, the way we
receive, the way we need.

MOTHER TERESA

One of life's greatest treasures is the love that binds hearts together
in friendship.

My purpose is that they may be encouraged in heart and united in
love, so that they may have the full riches of complete understanding,
in order that they may know the mystery of God, namely, Christ, in
whom are hidden all the treasures of wisdom and knowledge.

COLOSSIANS 2:2-3 NIV

Girliness is next to Godliness

Only He who created the wonders of the world entwines hearts in an eternal way.

God's Workmanship

Every time Jesus sees that there is a possibility of giving us more than we know how to ask for, He does so.

Ole Hallesby

For it is by grace you have been saved, through faith—and this not from yourselves, it is the gift of God—not by works, so that no one can boast. For we are God's workmanship, created in Christ Jesus to do good works, which God prepared in advance for us to do.

Ephesians 2:8-10 niv

Girliness is next to Godliness

As God's workmanship, we deserve to be treated, and to treat ourselves, with affection and affirmation, regardless of our appearance or performance.

Mary Ann Mayo

_____

_____

_____

_____

_____

_____

_____

_____

_____

Girliness is next to Godliness

Secret of Abundant Life

And this I pray, that your love may abound still more and more in real knowledge and all discernment, so that you may approve the things that are excellent, in order to be sincere and blameless until the day of Christ.

PHILIPPIANS 1:9-10 NASB

Not what we have but what we enjoy constitutes our abundance.

JOHN PETIT-SENN

God made you so you could share in His creation, could love and laugh and know Him.

TED GRIFFEN

Girliness is next to Godliness

To love by freely giving is its own reward. To be possessed by love and to in turn give love away is to find the secret of abundant life.

GLORIA GAITHER

Joy Personified

There is no greater joy nor greater reward than to make a fundamental difference in someone's life.

Mary Rose McGeady

For the Kingdom of God is not a matter of what we eat or drink, but of living a life of goodness and peace and joy in the Holy Spirit. If you serve Christ with this attitude, you will please God, and others will approve of you, too. So then, let us aim for harmony in the church and try to build each other up.

Romans 14:17-19 NLT

The sun does not shine for a few trees and flowers, but for the wide world's joy.

Henry Ward Beecher

Girliness is next to Godliness

As we grow in our capacities to see and enjoy the joys that God has placed in our lives, life becomes a glorious experience of discovering His endless wonders.

_____

_____

_____

_____

_____

_____

_____

_____

_____

_____

Girliness is next to Godliness

God's Heart

We think God's love rises and falls with our performance. It doesn't.... He loves you for whose you are: you are His child.

MAX LUCADO

Your life is a journey you must travel with a deep consciousness of God. It cost God plenty to get you out of that dead-end, empty-headed life you grew up in.... God always knew He was going to do this for you. It's because of this sacrificed Messiah...that you trust God, that you know you have a future in God.

1 PETER 1:18-21 THE MESSAGE

There is no need to plead that the love of God shall fill our hearts as though He were unwilling to fill us.... Love is pressing around us on all sides like air. Cease to resist it and instantly love takes possession.

AMY CARMICHAEL

Girliness is next to Godliness

*God's heart is the most sensitive and tender of all. No act
goes unnoticed, no matter how insignificant or small.*
RICHARD FOSTER

_____

_____

_____

_____

_____

_____

_____

_____

_____

_____

Treat Yourself

Besides the noble art of getting things done, there is a nobler art of leaving things undone. The wisdom of life consists in the elimination of nonessentials.

LIN YU-T'ANG

You wake up in the morning, and lo! your purse is magically filled with twenty-four hours of the magic tissue of the universe of your life. No one can take it from you. No one receives either more or less than you receive. Waste your infinitely precious commodity as much as you will, and the supply will never be withheld from you. Moreover, you cannot draw on the future. Impossible to get into debt. You can only w̶ ̶ ̶ ̶ ̶e passing movements. You cannot waste tomorrow. It is ̶ ̶ ̶ ̶ ̶r you.

ARNOLD BENNETT

Girliness is next to Godliness

Be kindly affectionate to one another with brotherly love, in honor giving preference to one another;...rejoicing in hope, patient in tribulation, continuing steadfastly in prayer; distributing to the needs of the saints, given to hospitality.

ROMANS 12:10-13 NKJV

_____

_____

_____

_____

_____

_____

_____

_____

_____

Happiness Is...

Your greatest pleasure is that which rebounds from hearts that you have made glad.

HENRY WARD BEECHER

Happiness can be thought, taught, and caught—but not bought.

Examine and see how good the Lord is. Happy is the person who trusts Him. You who belong to the Lord, fear Him! Those who fear Him will have everything they need.

PSALM 34:8-9 NCV

If nothing seems to go my way today, this is my happiness: God is my Father and I am His child.

BASILEA SCHLINK

Girliness is next to Godliness

An effort made for happiness of others lifts us above ourselves.
LYDIA MARIA CHILD

_____

_____

_____

_____

_____

_____

_____

_____

_____

_____

Girliness is next to Godliness

Sister Princesses

It's hard to be responsible, adult, and sensible all the time. How good it is to have a sister whose heart is as young as your own.

PAM BROWN

*You will also be a crown of beauty in the hand of the Lord,
And a royal diadem in the hand of your God.*

ISAIAH 62:3 NASB

Nothing's better than the wind to your back, the sun in front of you, and your friends beside you.

AARON DOUGLAS TRIMBLE

Two are better than one...for if they fall, one will lift up the other.

ECCLESIASTES 4:9-10 NRSV

Girliness is next to Godliness

She takes my hand and leads me along paths I would not have dared explore alone.
MAYA V. PATEL

_____

_____

_____

_____

_____

_____

_____

_____

_____

_____

Embraced by His Love

To be grateful is to recognize the love of God in everything He has given us—and He has given us everything. Every breath we draw is a gift of His love, every moment of existence a gift of grace.

THOMAS MERTON

God wants to continually add to us, to develop and enlarge us— always building on what He has already taught and built in us.

A. B. SIMPSON

You're blessed when you're at the end of your rope. With less of you there is more of God and His rule. You're blessed when you feel you've lost what is most dear to you. Only then can you be embraced by the One most dear to you.

MATTHEW 5:3-4 THE MESSAGE

Girliness is next to Godliness

God in His ample love embraces our love with...a sort of tenderness, and we must tread the Way to Him hand in hand.

SHELDON VANAUKEN

_____

_____

_____

_____

_____

_____

_____

_____

_____

_____

God Cares About Your Everythings

We are never more fulfilled than when our longing for God is met by His presence in our lives.

BILLY GRAHAM

The love of the Father is like a sudden rain shower that will pour forth when you least expect it, catching you up into wonder and praise.

RICHARD J. FOSTER

Your Father knows the things you need before you ask Him. So when you pray, you should pray like this: "Our Father in heaven, may Your name always be kept holy. May Your kingdom come and what You want be done, here on earth as it is in heaven."

MATTHEW 6:8-10 NCV

Girliness is next to Godliness

*Tuck [this] thought into your heart today. Treasure it. Your Father
God cares about your daily everythings that concern you.*
KAY ARTHUR

_____

_____

_____

_____

_____

_____

_____

_____

_____

_____

Everyday Is a Gift to Cherish

Everything in life is most fundamentally a gift. And you receive it best, and you live it best, by holding it with very open hands.

LEO O'DONOVAN

Go after a life of love as if your life depended on it—because it does. Give yourselves to the gifts God gives you. Most of all, try to proclaim His truth.

1 CORINTHIANS 14:1 THE MESSAGE

Time is a very precious gift of God; so precious that it's only given to us moment by moment.

AMELIA BARR

Girliness is next to Godliness

*Every day we live is a priceless gift of God, loaded with possibilities
to learn something new, to gain fresh insights.*
Dale Evans Rogers

_____

_____

_____

_____

_____

_____

_____

_____

_____

_____

_____

A Fountain of Gladness

When we do the best that we can, we never know what miracle is wrought in our life, or in the life of another.

HELEN KELLER

The wise are known for their understanding. Their pleasant words make them better teachers. Understanding is like a fountain which gives life to those who use it.

PROVERBS 16:21-22 NCV

Kindness has been described in many ways. It is the poetry of the heart, the music of the world. It is the golden chain which binds society together. It is a fountain of gladness.

THE WAR CRY

Girliness is next to Godliness

A kind heart is a fountain of gladness, making
everything in its vicinity freshen into smiles.
WASHINGTON IRVING

Girliness is next to Godliness

What Women Want

It is an extraordinary and beautiful thing that God, in creation...
works with the beauty of matter; the reality of things; the
discoveries of the senses, all five of them; so that we, in turn, may
hear the grass growing; see a face springing to life in love and
laughter.... The offerings of creation...our glimpses of truth.

MADELIENE L'ENGLE

Show me the right path, O Lord;
point out the road for me to follow.
Lead me by Your truth and teach me,
for You are the God who saves me.
All day long I put my hope in You.

PSALM 25:4-5 NLT

Girliness is next to Godliness

In the end, I think this is what women truly desire: to know God and to stand tall in their faith, strong at the core, tender in heart.
RUTH SENTER

Blessings Await

Having someone who understands is a great blessing for ourselves. Being someone who understands is a great blessing to others.

JANETTE OKE

Lift up your eyes. Your heavenly Father waits to bless you—in inconceivable ways to make your life what you never dreamed it could be.

ANNE ORTLUND

God can pour on the blessings in astonishing ways so that you're ready for anything and everything, more than just ready to do what needs to be done.

2 CORINTHIANS 9:8 THE MESSAGE

Girliness is next to Godliness

*Some blessings—like rainbows after rain or a friend's listening ear—
are extraordinary gifts waiting to be discovered in an ordinary day.*

He Is Faithful

For the word of the Lord is upright,
And all His work is done in faithfulness.
He loves righteousness and justice;
The earth is full of the lovingkindness of the Lord.

PSALM 33:4-5 NASB

Not everyone possesses boundless energy or a conspicuous talent.
We are not equally blessed with great intellect or physical beauty or
emotional strength. But we have all been given the same ability to
be faithful.

GIGI GRAHAM TCHIVIDJIAN

Girliness is next to Godliness

If you have a special need today, focus your full attention on the goodness and greatness of your Father rather than on the size of your need. Your need is so small compared to His ability to meet it.

_____

_____

_____

_____

_____

_____

_____

_____

_____

_____

A Countenance Is Made Beautiful

Joy is the echo of God's life within us.

JOSEPH MARMION

God has made everything beautiful for its own time. He has planted eternity in the human heart.

ECCLESIASTES 3:11 NLT

The beauty of the earth, the beauty of the sky, the order of the stars, the sun, the moon...their very loveliness is their confession of God: for who made these lovely mutable things, but He who is Himself unchangeable beauty?

AUGUSTINE

Think of all the beauty still left around you and be happy.

ANNE FRANK

Girliness is next to Godliness

As a countenance is made beautiful by the soul's shining through it, so the world is beautiful by the shining through it of God.

FRIEDRICH HEINRICH JACOBI

God Loves to Hear Us Laugh

There is no duty we so much underrate as the duty of being happy.
By being happy, we sow anonymous benefits upon the world.

ROBERT LOUIS STEVENSON

And now, God, do it again—
bring rains to our drought-stricken lives
So those who planted their crops in despair
will shout hurrahs at the harvest,
So those who went off with heavy hearts
will come home laughing, with armloads of blessing.

PSALM 126:3-5 THE MESSAGE

God is at home in the play of His children. He loves to hear us laugh.

PETER MARSHALL

Girliness is next to Godliness

She is clothed with strength and dignity; she can laugh at the days to come.

PROVERBS 31:25 NIV

_____

_____

_____

_____

_____

_____

_____

_____

_____

_____

Treasure Today

See each morning a world made anew, as if it were the morning of the very first day;...treasure and use it, as if it were the final hour of the very last day.

FAY HARTZELL ARNOLD

For the Lord grants wisdom!
From His mouth come knowledge and understanding.
He grants a treasure of common sense to the honest.
He is a shield to those who walk with integrity.
He guards the paths of the just
    and protects those who are faithful to Him.
Then you will understand what is right, just, and fair,
    and you will find the right way to go.

PROVERBS 2:5-9 NLT

Normal day, let me be aware of the treasure you are. Let me learn from you, love you, bless you before you depart. Let me not pass you by in quest of some rare and perfect tomorrow.

Girliness is next to Godliness

In ordinary life we hardly realize that we receive a great deal more than we give, and that it is only with gratitude that life becomes rich.
DIETRICH BONHOEFFER

_____

_____

_____

_____

_____

_____

_____

_____

_____

_____

Seriously?!

I am hereby officially tendering my resignation as an adult. I have decided I would like to accept the responsibilities of an 8 year-old again.... I want to believe in the power of smiles, hugs, a kind word, truth, justice, peace, dreams, the imagination, mankind, and making angels in the snow. So...here's my checkbook, my car keys, and my credit card bills.... And if you want to discuss this further, you'll have to catch me first, 'cause... "Tag! You're it."

It pays to take life seriously;
things work out when you trust in God.

PROVERBS 16:20 THE MESSAGE

Girliness is next to Godliness

The purpose of life is to fight maturity.
DICK WERTHIMER

_____

_____

_____

_____

_____

_____

_____

_____

_____

_____

_____

Simple and Natural Things

The splendor of the rose and the whiteness of the lily do not rob the little violet of its scent nor the daisy of its simple charm. If every tiny flower wanted to be a rose, spring would lose its loveliness.

THÉRÈSE OF LISIEUX

I'm asking God for one thing,
only one thing:
To live with Him in His house
my whole life long.
I'll contemplate His beauty;
I'll study at His feet.
That's the only quiet, secure place
in a noisy world.

PSALM 27:4-5 THE MESSAGE

Happy people...enjoy the fundamental, often very simple things of life.... They savor the moment, glad to be alive, enjoying their work, their families, the good things around them. They are adaptable; they can bend with the wind, adjust to the changes in their times, enjoy the contest of life.... Their eyes are turned outward; they are aware, compassionate.
They have the capacity to love.

JANE CANFIELD

Girliness is next to Godliness

From the simple seeds of understanding, we reap the lovely harvest of true friendship.

_____

_____

_____

_____

_____

_____

_____

_____

_____

_____

A Feeling that Nurtures the Soul

*Can you see the holiness in those things you take for granted—a
paved road or a washing machine? If you concentrate on finding
what is good in every situation, you will discover that your life will
suddenly be filled with gratitude, a feeling that nurtures the soul.*

HAROLD KUSHNER

*It is good to give thanks to the Lord
And to sing praises to Your name, O Most High;
To declare Your lovingkindness in the morning
And Your faithfulness by night,*

PSALM 92:1-2 NASB

*Gratitude. More aware of what you have than what you don't.
Recognizing the treasure in the simple—a child's hug, fertile soil, a
golden sunset. Relishing in the comfort of the common—a warm
bed, a hot meal, a clean shirt.*

MAX LUCADO

Girliness is next to Godliness

Gratitude is not only the greatest of virtues, but the parent of all others.
CICERO

_____

_____

_____

_____

_____

_____

_____

_____

_____

_____

The Element of Joy

Into all our lives, in many simple, familiar, homely ways,
God infuses this element of joy from the surprises of life that
unexpectedly brighten our days and fill our eyes with light.

HENRY WADSWORTH LONGFELLOW

A joyful heart is like a sunshine of God's love, the hope of eternal
happiness, a burning flame of God.... And if we pray, we will
become that sunshine of God's love—in our own home, the place
where we live, and in the world at large.

MOTHER TERESA

A good laugh is as good as a prayer sometimes.

LUCY MAUD MONTGOMERY

Girliness is next to Godliness

He will yet fill your mouth with laughter and your lips with shouts of joy.
JOB 8:21 NIV

_____

_____

_____

_____

_____

_____

_____

_____

_____

_____

Share the Secret

The real secret of happiness is not what you give or what you receive, it's what you share.

Know that I'm on your side, right alongside you. You're not in this alone. I want you woven into a tapestry of love, in touch with everything there is to know of God. Then you will have minds confident and at rest, focused on Christ, God's great mystery. All the richest treasures of wisdom and knowledge are embedded in that mystery and nowhere else.

COLOSSIANS 2:1-2 THE MESSAGE

The secret of life is that all we have and are is a gift of grace to be shared.

LLOYD JOHN OGILVIE

Girliness is next to Godliness

To be able to find joy in another's joy, that is the secret of happiness.

_____

_____

_____

_____

_____

_____

_____

_____

_____

_____

Created to Love

Love loves to be told what it knows already.... It wants to be asked for what it longs to give.

PETER TAYLOR FORSYTH

Let love be genuine; hate what is evil, hold fast to what is good; love one another with mutual affection; outdo one another in showing honor.

ROMANS 12:9-10 NRSV

Who we are is connected to those we love and to those who have influenced us toward goodness.

CHRISTOPHER DE VINCK

Girliness is next to Godliness

Caring words, friendship, affectionate touch—all of these have a healing
quality. Why? Because we were all created by God to give and receive love.

JACK FROST

How High Our Dreams Can Soar

God's gifts put man's best dreams to shame.

ELIZABETH BARRETT BROWNING

Allow your dreams a place in your prayers and plans. God-given dreams can help you move into the future He is preparing for you.

BARBARA JOHNSON

More things are wrought by prayer
Than this world dreams of.

ALFRED, LORD TENNYSON

God can do anything, you know—far more than you could ever imagine or guess or request in your wildest dreams! He does it...by working within us, His Spirit deeply and gently within us.

EPHESIANS 3:20 THE MESSAGE

Girliness is next to Godliness

The stars exist that we might know how high our dreams can soar.

_____

_____

_____

_____

_____

_____

_____

_____

_____

_____

God's Wonderful Plan

Stand outside this evening. Look at the stars. Know that you are special and loved by the One who created them.

> Put God in charge of your work,
> then what you've planned will take place....
> We plan the way we want to live,
> but only God makes us able to live it.

PROVERBS 16:3, 9 THE MESSAGE

God created the universe, but He also created you. God knows you, God loves you, and God cares about the tiniest details of your life.

BRUCE BICKEL AND STAN JANTZ

Girliness is next to Godliness

God has a wonderful plan for each person.... He knew even before He created this world what beauty He would bring forth from our lives.

LOUIS B. WYLY

_____

_____

_____

_____

_____

_____

_____

_____

_____

_____

Expectations and Memories

Every day in a life fills the whole life with expectation and memory.

C. S. LEWIS

When I stand before God at the end of my life, I would hope that I would not have a single bit of talent left and could say, "I used everything You gave me."

ERMA BOMBECK

Though He knows the name of every star and His kingdom spans galaxies, God delights in being a part of our lives.

JOHN ELDREDGE

He made the entire human race and made the earth hospitable, with plenty of time and space for living so we could seek after God, and not just grope around in the dark but actually find Him.... He's not remote; he's near.

ACTS 17:26-27 THE MESSAGE

What we have once enjoyed we can never lose. All that we love deeply becomes a part of us.

HELEN KELLER

Girliness is next to Godliness

*Once we discover how to appreciate the timeless values in our
daily experiences, we can enjoy the best things in life.*

HARRY HEPNER

_____

_____

_____

_____

_____

_____

_____

_____

_____

_____

God Knows You

God not only knows us, but He values us highly in spite of all He knows.... You and I are the creatures He prizes above the rest of His creation. We are made in His image and He sacrificed His Son that each one of us might be one with Him.

JOHN FISHER

O Lord, You have examined my heart
and know everything about me.
You know when I sit down or stand up.
You know my thoughts even when I'm far away.
You see me when I travel
and when I rest at home.
You know everything I do.
You know what I am going to say....
You go before me and follow me.
You place your hand of blessing on my head.

PSALM 139:1-5 NLT

Girliness is next to Godliness

God knows everything about us. And He cares about everything. Moreover, He can manage every situation. And He loves us! Surely this is enough to open the wellsprings of joy.... And joy is always a source of strength.
HANNAH WHITALL SMITH

_____

_____

_____

_____

_____

_____

_____

_____

_____

Girliness is next to Godliness

Love Wrapped Up for You

To receive a gift, molded from love and sacrifice, selected with care and tied up with all the excitement the giver has to offer, is indeed rare. They don't come along often, but when they do, cherish them.

ERMA BOMBECK

But me He caught—reached all the way
from sky to sea; He pulled me out
Of that ocean of hate, that enemy chaos,
the void in which I was drowning.
They hit me when I was down,
but God stuck by me.
He stood me up on a wide-open field;
I stood there saved—surprised to be loved!

PSALM 18:18-19 THE MESSAGE

Girliness is next to Godliness

Each day is a treasure box of gifts from God, just waiting to be opened. Open your gifts with excitement. You will find forgiveness attached to ribbons of joy. You will find love wrapped in sparkling gems.

JOAN CLAYTON

_____

_____

_____

_____

_____

_____

_____

_____

_____

Truly You

Keep your head and your heart going in the right direction and you'll not have to worry about your feet.

Greatness lies not in being strong, but in the right use of strength.

HENRY WARD BEECHER

I pray that from His glorious, unlimited resources He will empower you with inner strength through His Spirit. Then Christ will make His home in your hearts as you trust in Him. Your roots will grow down into God's love and keep you strong.

EPHESIANS 3:16-17 NLT

What is strength without a double share of wisdom?

JOHN MILTON

Girliness is next to Godliness

What lies behind us and what lies before us are tiny matters compared to what lies within us.
RALPH WALDO EMERSON

_____

_____

_____

_____

_____

_____

_____

_____

_____

_____

_____

_____

_____

Girliness is next to Godliness

God's Special Work of Art

Live out your God-created identity. Live generously and graciously toward others, the way God lives toward you.

MATTHEW 5:48 THE MESSAGE

Remember you are very special to God and His precious child. He has promised to complete the good work He has begun in you. As you continue to grow in Him, He will teach you to be a blessing to others.

GARY SMALLEY AND JOHN TRENT

Thank You for making me so wonderfully complex! Your workmanship is marvelous—how well I know it.

PSALM 139:14 NLT

Girliness is next to Godliness

Each one of us is God's special work of art. Through us, He teaches and inspires,
delights and encourages, informs and uplifts all those who view our lives.
JONI EARECKSON TADA

What Is Essential

It is only with the heart that one can see rightly. What is essential is invisible to the eye.

ANTOINE DE SAINT-EXUPÉRY

You're blessed when you get your inside world—your mind and heart—put right. Then you can see God in the outside world.

MATTHEW 5:8 THE MESSAGE

Nothing is so strong as gentleness, and nothing so gentle as real strength.

FRANÇOIS DE SALES

Pursue righteousness, godliness, faith, love, endurance and gentleness. Fight the good fight of the faith. Take hold of the eternal life to which you were called when you made your good confession in the presence of many witnesses.

1 TIMOTHY 6:11-12 NIV

Girliness is next to Godliness

The human contribution is the essential ingredient. It is only in the giving of oneself to others that we truly live.
ETHEL PERCY ANDRUS

_____

_____

_____

_____

_____

_____

_____

_____

_____

Girliness is next to Godliness

Prayer Power

One single grateful thought raised to heaven is the most perfect prayer.

G. E. LESSING

The prayer that is said with faith will make the sick person well; the Lord will heal that person. And if the person has sinned, the sins will be forgiven. Confess your sins to each other and pray for each other so God can heal you. When a believing person prays, great things happen.

JAMES 5:15-16 NCV

Do not pray for easy lives. Pray to be stronger.... Do not pray for tasks equal to your powers. Pray for powers equal to your tasks. Then the doing of your work shall be no miracle, but you shall be the miracle.

PHILLIPS BROOKS

Girliness is next to Godliness

Your life is the answer to someone's prayers.

_____

_____

_____

_____

_____

_____

_____

_____

_____

_____

_____

The Attention of God

God is every moment totally aware of each one of us. Totally aware in intense concentration and love.... No one passes through any area of life, happy or tragic, without the attention of God.

EUGENIA PRICE

May you have the power to understand, as all God's people should, how wide, how long, how high, and how deep His love is.

EPHESIANS 3:18 NLT

God may not provide us with a perfectly ordered life, but what He does provide is Himself, His presence, and open doors that bring us closer to being productive, positive and realistic Christian women.

JUDITH BRILES

Girliness is next to Godliness

We have been in God's thought from all eternity,
and in His creative love, His attention never leaves us.
MICHAEL QUOIST

_____

_____

_____

_____

_____

_____

_____

_____

_____

Girliness is next to Godliness

Work-out, Smirk-out

*I think that anyone who comes upon a Nautilus machine suddenly
will agree with me that its prototype was clearly invented at
some time in history when torture was considered a reasonable
alternative to diplomacy.*

ANNA QUINDLEN

*As pressure and stress bear down on me,
I find joy in Your commands.*

PSALM 119:143 NLT

*Mach-S, the speed at which stress can't keep up, is simply forward
motion. But it has to be self-propelled. Note that people in cars are
still stressed.*

JEF MALLETT,

Dig where the gold is…unless you just need some exercise.

JOHN M. CAPOZZI

Girliness is next to Godliness

I believe that every human has a finite number of heart-beats. I don't intend to waste any of mine running around doing exercises.
BUZZ ALDRIN

Girliness is next to Godliness

A Smile Costs Nothing

A smile costs nothing but gives much. It takes but a moment, and the memory of it sometimes lasts forever.

A happy heart makes the face cheerful.

PROVERBS 15:13 NIV

We have something very precious. I am reminded of that whenever I am away from you busy doing something and you drift into my mind, making me smile inside.

GARRY LAFOLLETTE

A smile is a curve that sets everything straight.

PHYLLIS DILLER

Whole-hearted, ready laughter heals, encourages, relaxes anyone within hearing distance. The laughter that springs from love makes wide the space around—gives room for the loved one to enter in.

EUGENIA PRICE

Girliness is next to Godliness

A smile is a light in the window of the soul indicating that the heart is at home.

_____

_____

_____

_____

_____

_____

_____

_____

_____

_____

Girliness is next to Godliness

Think About Such Things

It is not my business to think about myself. My business is to think about God. It is for God to think about me.

Simone Weil

Whatever is true, whatever is noble, whatever is right, whatever is pure, whatever is lovely, whatever is admirable—if anything is excellent or praiseworthy—think about such things.

Philippians 4:8 niv

We must not, in trying to think about how we can make a big difference, ignore the small daily differences we can make which, over time, add up to big differences that we often cannot foresee.

Marian Wright Edelman

Girliness is next to Godliness

As a rose fills a room with its fragrance, so will God's love fill our lives.
MARGARET BROWNLEY

Attitude Is Everything

If you have any encouragement from being united with Christ, if any comfort from His love, if any fellowship with the Spirit, if any tenderness and compassion, then make my joy complete by being like-minded, having the same love, being one in spirit and purpose. Do nothing out of selfish ambition or vain conceit, but in humility consider others better than yourselves.

PHILIPPIANS 2:1-3 NIV

A positive attitude may not solve all your problems, but it will annoy enough people to make it worth the effort.

HERM ALBRIGHT

Girliness is next to Godliness

A strong positive mental attitude will create more miracles than any wonder drug.
PATRICIA NEAL

Love Conquers All

Love grows from our capacity to give what is deepest within ourselves and also receive what is the deepest within another person. The heart becomes an ocean strong and deep, launching all on its tide.

For great is His love toward us, and the faithfulness of the Lord endures forever.

PSALM 117:2 NIV

Love is that condition in which the happiness of another person is essential to your own.

ROBERT A. HEINLEIN

Before anything else, above all else, beyond everything else, God loves us. God loves us extravagantly, ridiculously, without limit or condition. God is in love with us...God yearns for us.

ROBERTA BONDI

Girliness is next to Godliness

God has called us into the joyous ministry of giving His love away to others.
DON LESSIN

Body and Spirit

We must drink deeply from the very Source the deep calm and peace of interior quietude and refreshment of God, allowing the pure water of divine grace to flow plentifully and unceasingly from the Source itself.

Mother Teresa

Don't depend on your own wisdom. Respect the Lord and refuse to do wrong. Then your body will be healthy, and your bones will be strong. Honor the Lord with your wealth and the firstfruits from all your crops. Then your barns will be full, and your wine barrels will overflow with new wine.

Proverbs 3:7-10 NCV

What you do when you don't have to determines what you will be when you can no longer help it.

Rudyard Kipling

Girliness is next to Godliness

True silence is the rest of the mind; it is to the spirit what sleep is to the body,
nourishment and refreshment.
WILLIAM PENN

_____

_____

_____

_____

_____

_____

_____

_____

_____

_____

The One and Only You

You have a unique message to deliver, a unique song to sing, a unique act of love to bestow. This message, this song, and this act of love have been entrusted exclusively to the one and only you.

JOHN POWELL

Oh God, You have given me...a life of clay. Put Your big hands around mine and guide my hands so that every time I make a mark on this life, it will be Your mark.

GLORIA GAITHER

The Lord will guide you always; He will satisfy your needs in a sun-scorched land.... You will be like a well-watered garden, like a spring whose waters never fail.

ISAIAH 58:11 NIV

Girliness is next to Godliness

*When we allow God the privilege of shaping our lives,
we discover new depths of purpose and meaning.*
JONI EARECKSON TADA

_____

_____

_____

_____

_____

_____

_____

_____

_____

_____

Simple Tastes, Inside and Out

Eat breakfast like a king, lunch like a prince, and dinner like a pauper.

ADELLE DAVIS

Don't fuss about what's on the table at mealtimes or if the clothes in your closet are in fashion. There is far more to your inner life than the food you put in your stomach, more to your outer appearance than the clothes you hang on your body. Look at the ravens, free and unfettered, not tied down to a job description, carefree in the care of God. And you count far more.

LUKE 12:22-24 THE MESSAGE

Cultivation of the mind is as necessary as food to the body.

CICERO

Girliness is next to Godliness

Prayer is to the spirit what breath is to the body. We treat prayer as though it
were the spice of life, but the Bible prescribes it as a vital staple in our diet.
DAVID HUBBARD

_____

_____

_____

_____

_____

_____

_____

_____

_____

_____

The Generous Spirit

You must give some time to your fellow men. Even if it's a little thing, do something for others—something for which you get no pay but the privilege of doing it.

ALBERT SCHWEITZER

Give what you have. To someone, it may be better than you dare to think.

HENRY WADSWORTH LONGFELLOW

When you give a lunch or a dinner, don't invite only your friends, your family, your other relatives, and your rich neighbors. At another time they will invite you to eat with them, and you will be repaid. Instead, when you give a feast, invite the poor, the crippled, the lame, and the blind. Then you will be blessed, because they have nothing and cannot pay you back.

LUKE 14:12-14 NCV

Make all you can, save all you can, give all you can.

JOHN WESLEY

Girliness is next to Godliness

We make a living by what we get, we make a life by what we give.
SIR WINSTON CHURCHILL

_____

_____

_____

_____

_____

_____

_____

_____

_____

_____

Our Significant Place in this World

As women, we want to know we are important and that we have a significant place in our world. We need to know that we matter to someone, that our lives are making a difference in the lives of other people, that we are able to touch their souls. This desire to have value is God-given.

BEVERLY LAHAYE

Eating lunch with a friend. Trying to do a decent day's work. Hearing the rain patter against the window. There is no event so commonplace but that God is present within it, always hiddenly, always leaving you room to recognize Him or not to recognize Him.

FREDERICK BUECHNER

Girliness is next to Godliness

In all your ways acknowledge Him, and He shall direct your paths.
PROVERBS 3:6 NKJV

_____

_____

_____

_____

_____

_____

_____

_____

_____

_____

Slow Down and Enjoy Life

Slow down awhile! Push aside the press of the immediate. Take time today, if only for a moment, to lovingly encourage each one in your family.

GARY SMALLEY AND JOHN TRENT

Dear friend, I pray that you may enjoy good health and that all may go well with you, even as your soul is getting along well.

3 JOHN 1:2 NIV

Many persons have a wrong idea of what constitutes true happiness. It is not attained through self-gratification but through fidelity to a worthy purpose.

HELEN KELLER

Most folks are about as happy as they make up their minds to be.

ABRAHAM LINCOLN

Girliness is next to Godliness

Slow down and enjoy life. It's not only the scenery you miss by going too fast—you also miss the sense of where you are going and why.
EDDIE CANTOR

_____

_____

_____

_____

_____

_____

_____

_____

_____

_____

A Love Letter from God

God is so big He can cover the whole world with His love, and so small He can curl up inside your heart.

JUNE MASTERS BACHER

The Lord your God is with you....
He will take great delight in you,
He will quiet you with His love,
He will rejoice over you with singing.

ZEPHANIAH 3:17 NIV

Are you aware that the Father takes delight in you and that He thinks about you all the time?

JACK FROST

Girliness is next to Godliness

All the things in this world are gifts and signs of God's love to us. The whole world is a love letter from God.
PETER KREEFT

The Art of Courage

Courage is doing what you're afraid to do. There can be no courage unless you're scared.

Eddie Rickenbacker

Courage is the art of being the only one who knows you're scared to death.

Harold Wilson

This is my command—be strong and courageous! Do not be afraid or discouraged. For the Lord your God is with you wherever you go.

Joshua 1:9 nlt

I wanted you to see what real courage is.... It's when you know you're licked before you begin but you begin anyway and you see it through no matter what.

Harper Lee

The only courage that matters is the kind that gets you from one moment to the next.

Mignon McLaughlin,

Girliness is next to Godliness

Courage is fear that has said its prayers.
DOROTHY BERNARD

Mini-Vacations

Women of adventure have conquered their fates and know how to live exciting and fulfilling lives right where they are. They have learned to reinvent themselves and find creative ways to enjoy the world and their place in it. They know how to take mini-vacations, stop and smell the roses, and live fully in the moment.

BARBARA JENKINS

I know the Lord is always with me.
I will not be shaken, for He is right beside me.
No wonder my heart is glad, and I rejoice.
My body rests in safety.

PSALM 16:8-9 NLT

Girliness is next to Godliness

Happiness turns up more or less where you'd expect it to be—a good marriage, a rewarding job, a pleasant vacation. Joy, on the other hand, is as notoriously unpredictable as the One who bequeaths it.

FREDERICK BUECHNER

_____

_____

_____

_____

_____

_____

_____

_____

_____

Kaleidoscope of New Possibilities

There are no limits to our opportunities. Most of us see only a small portion of what is possible. We create opportunities by seeing the possibilities and having the persistence to act upon them. We must always remember...opportunities are always here, but we must look for them.

Happy are those who hear the joyful call to worship,
for they will walk in the light of Your presence, Lord.
They rejoice all day long in Your wonderful reputation.
They exult in Your righteousness.
You are their glorious strength.
It pleases You to make us strong.

PSALM 89:15-17 NLT

Remember that happiness is a way of travel—not a destination.

ROY M. GOODMAN

Girliness is next to Godliness

*You see things as they are and ask, "Why?" I dream
things as they never were and ask, "Why not?"*
GEORGE BERNARD SHAW

_____

_____

_____

_____

_____

_____

_____

_____

_____

_____

Hope for Today

Hope begins in the dark, the stubborn hope that if you just show up and try to do the right thing, the dawn will come. You wait and watch and work: You don't give up.

ANNE LAMOTT

This I call to mind and therefore I have hope: Because of the Lord's great love we are not consumed, for His compassions never fail. They are new every morning; great is Your faithfulness.

LAMENTATIONS 3:21-23 NCV

Do not spoil what you have by desiring what you have not; but remember that what you now have was once among the things you only hoped for.

EPICURUS

Girliness is next to Godliness

*It is difficult to say what is impossible, for the dream of
yesterday is the hope of today and the reality of tomorrow.*
ROBERT H. GODDARD

Girliness is next to Godliness

The Ocean of God's Love

May God give you eyes to see beauty only the heart can understand.

God loves you in the morning sun and the evening rain, without caution or regret.

BRENNAN MANNING

And I am convinced that nothing can ever separate us from God's love. Neither death nor life, neither angels nor demons, neither our fears for today nor our worries about tomorrow—not even the powers of hell can separate us from God's love. No power in the sky above or in the earth below—indeed, nothing in all creation will ever be able to separate us from the love of God that is revealed in Christ Jesus our Lord.

ROMANS 8:38-39 NLT

God will never let you be shaken or moved from your place near His heart.

JONI EARECKSON TADA

Girliness is next to Godliness

The treasure our heart searches for is found in the ocean of God's love.
JANET WEAVER SMITH

Real Joy

May the God of hope fill you with all joy and peace as you trust in Him, so that you may overflow with hope.

ROMANS 15:13 NIV

I've grown to realize the joy that comes from little victories is preferable to the fun that comes from ease and the pursuit of pleasure.

LAWANA BLACKWELL,

Joyful are people of integrity,
who follow the instructions of the Lord.
Joyful are those who obey His laws
and search for Him with all their hearts.

PSALM 119:1-2 NLT

Girliness is next to Godliness

*Real joy comes not from ease or riches or from the
praise of men, but from doing something worthwhile.*
SIR WILFRED GRENFELL

_____

_____

_____

_____

_____

_____

_____

_____

_____

_____

_____

Little Things Mean a Lot

I wished I had a box, the biggest I could find,
I'd fill it right up to the brim with everything that's kind.
A box without a lock, of course, and never any key;
for everything inside that box would then be offered free.
Grateful words for joys received I'd freely give away.
Oh, let us open wide a box of praise for every day.

Whoever can be trusted with very little can also be trusted with much, and whoever is dishonest with very little will also be dishonest with much.

LUKE 16:10 NIV

Half the joy of life is in little things taken on the run. Let us run if we must—even the sands do that—but let us keep our hearts young and our eyes open that nothing worth our while shall escape us. And everything is worth its while if we only grasp it and its significance.

VICTOR CHERBULIEZ

Girliness is next to Godliness

Little things seem nothing, but they give peace, like those meadow flowers which individually seem odorless but all together perfume the air.
GEORGES BERNANOS

Love Isn't Love 'til You Give It Away

You're here to be light, bringing out the God-colors in the world. God is not a secret to be kept. We're going public with this, as public as a city on a hill. If I make you light-bearers, you don't think I'm going to hide you under a bucket, do you? I'm putting you on a light stand. Now that I've put you there on a hilltop, on a light stand—shine! Keep open house; be generous with your lives. By opening up to others, you'll prompt people to open up with God, this generous Father in heaven.

MATTHEW 5:14 THE MESSAGE

The true meaning of life is to plant trees, under whose shade you do not expect to sit.

NELSON HENDERSON

Girliness is next to Godliness

Love in the heart wasn't put there to stay;
Love isn't love 'til you give it away.
OSCAR HAMMERSTEIN II

_____

_____

_____

_____

_____

_____

_____

_____

_____

_____

You Are God's Created Beauty

Then God said, "Let us make man in our image, in our likeness, and let them rule over the fish of the sea and the birds of the air, over the livestock, over all the earth, and over all the creatures that move along the ground." So God created man in His own image, in the image of God He created him; male and female He created them.

GENESIS 1:26-27 NIV

Beauty is not caused. It is.

EMILY DICKINSON

In all ranks of life the human heart yearns for the beautiful, and the beautiful things that God makes are His gift to all alike.

HARRIET BEECHER STOWE

Girliness is next to Godliness

You are God's created beauty and the focus of His affection and delight.
JANET WEAVER SMITH

_____

_____

_____

_____

_____

_____

_____

_____

_____

_____

Making a Difference

Character is like a tree and reputation like its shadow. The shadow is what we think of it; the tree is the real thing.

ABRAHAM LINCOLN

We can rejoice, too, when we run into problems and trials, for we know that they help us develop endurance. And endurance develops strength of character, and character strengthens our confident hope of salvation. And this hope will not lead to disappointment. For we know how dearly God loves us, because He has given us the Holy Spirit to fill our hearts with His love.

ROMANS 5:3-5 NLT

Personality can open doors, but only character can keep them open.

ELMER G. LETTERMAN

Character cannot be developed in ease and quiet. Only through experience of trial and suffering can the soul be strengthened, ambition inspired, and success achieved.

HELEN KELLER

Girliness is next to Godliness

People grow through experience if they meet life honestly
and courageously. This is how character is built.
ELEANOR ROOSEVELT

_____

_____

_____

_____

_____

_____

_____

_____

_____

_____

Girliness is next to Godliness

The Inner Sanctuary
of the Soul

Isn't it a wonderful morning? The world looks like something God had just imagined for His own pleasure.

LUCY MAUD MONTGOMERY

One can get just as much exultation in losing oneself in a little thing as in a big thing. It is nice to think how one can be recklessly lost in a daisy!

ANNE MORROW LINDBERGH

What marvelous love the Father has extended to us! Just look at it—we're called children of God! That's who we really are.

1 JOHN 3:1 THE MESSAGE

Girliness is next to Godliness

God waits for us in the inner sanctuary of the soul. He welcomes us there.
RICHARD J. FOSTER

_____

_____

_____

_____

_____

_____

_____

_____

_____

_____

The Treasure of Kindness

The ideals which have lighted my way, and time after time have given me new courage to face life cheerfully, have been Kindness, Beauty, and Truth.

ALBERT EINSTEIN

Never let loyalty and kindness leave you!...
Write them deep within your heart.
Then you will find favor with both God and people,
and you will earn a good reputation.

PROVERBS 3:3-4 NLT

Kindness is the only service that will stand the storm of life and not wash out. It will wear well and be remembered long after the prism of politeness or the complexion of courtesy has faded away. When I am gone, I hope it can be said of me that I plucked a thistle and planted a flower wherever I thought a flower would grow.

Girliness is next to Godliness

I expect to pass through this world but once; any good thing therefore that I can do, or any kindness that I can show to any fellow creature, let me do it now; let me not defer or neglect it, for I shall not pass this way again.
STEPHEN GRELLET

_____

_____

_____

_____

_____

_____

_____

_____

_____

Spending Time

An unhurried sense of time is in itself a form of wealth.

BONNIE FRIEDMAN

When the most important things in our life happen we quite often do not know, at the moment, what is going on.

C. S. LEWIS

To everything there is a season,
A time for every purpose under heaven.

ECCLESIASTES 3:1 NKJV

Time is the coin of your life. It is the only coin you have, and only you can determine how it will be spent. Be careful lest you let other people spend it for you.

CARL SANDBURG

Girliness is next to Godliness

This time, like all times, is a very good one, if we but know what to do with it.
RALPH WALDO EMERSON

_____

_____

_____

_____

_____

_____

_____

_____

_____

_____

Girliness is next to Godliness

You Are Incomparable

Since this is the kind of life we have chosen, the life of the Spirit, let us make sure that we do not just hold it as an idea in our heads or a sentiment in our hearts, but work out its implications in every detail of our lives. That means we will not compare ourselves with each other as if one of us were better and another worse. We have far more interesting things to do with our lives. Each of us is an original.

GALATIANS 5:25-26 THE MESSAGE

I know not where His islands lift
their fronded palms in air;
I only know I cannot drift
beyond His love and care.

JOHN GREENLEAF WHITTIER

Girliness is next to Godliness

*Since you are like no other being ever created since
the beginning of time, you are incomparable.*
BRENDA UELAND

Natural Wonders

If we are cheerful and contented, all nature smiles...the flowers are more fragrant, the birds sing more sweetly, and the sun, moon, and stars all appear more beautiful and seem to rejoice with us.

ORISON SWETT MARDEN

What a wildly wonderful world, God! You made it all, with Wisdom at Your side, made earth overflow with Your wonderful creations.... All the creatures look expectantly to You to give them their meals on time. You come, and they gather around; You open Your hand and they eat from it.... Take back Your Spirit and they die, revert to original mud; Send out Your Spirit and they spring to life.

PSALM 104:24-30 THE MESSAGE

Girliness is next to Godliness

Beauty puts a face on God. When we gaze at nature, at a loved one, at a work of art, our soul immediately recognizes and is drawn to the face of God.
MARGARET BROWNLEY

_____

_____

_____

_____

_____

_____

_____

_____

_____

_____

Girliness is next to Godliness

That's What Little Girls Are Made Of

A little girl is...innocence playing in the mud, beauty standing on its head, and motherhood dragging a doll by the foot.

ALAN BECK

Don't be concerned about the outward beauty of fancy hairstyles, expensive jewelry, or beautiful clothes. You should clothe yourselves instead with the beauty that comes from within, the unfading beauty of a gentle and quiet spirit, which is so precious to God.

1 PETER 3:3-4 NLT

Above the place where children play
A window opens, far away,
For God to hear the happy noise
Made by His little girls and boys.

CHARLES DALMON

Girliness is next to Godliness

What are little girls made of?
Sugar and spice and all things nice.
That's what little girls are made of.

Girliness is next to Godliness

Sunshine and Smiles

One day spent in Your house, this beautiful place of worship, beats thousands spent on Greek island beaches.... All sunshine and sovereign is God, generous in gifts and glory.

PSALM 84:10-11 THE MESSAGE

A smile takes but a moment, but its effects sometimes last forever.

J. E. SMITH

I am still determined to be cheerful and happy, in whatever situation I may be; for I have also learned from experience that the greater part of our happiness or misery depends upon our dispositions, and not upon our circumstances.

MARTHA WASHINGTON

Girliness is next to Godliness

What sunshine is to flowers, smiles are to humanity. These are but trifles, to be sure; but, scattered along life's pathway, the good they do is inconceivable.
JOSEPH ADDISON

_____

_____

_____

_____

_____

_____

_____

_____

_____

_____

Nature's Treasure

"Just living is not enough," said the butterfly. "One must have sunshine, freedom, and a little flower."

HANS CHRISTIAN ANDERSEN

If we are children of God, we have a tremendous treasure in nature and will realize that it is holy and sacred. We will see God reaching out to us in every wind that blows, every sunrise and sunset, every cloud in the sky, every flower that blooms, and every leaf that fades.

OSWALD CHAMBERS

If anyone belongs to Christ, there is a new creation. The old things have gone; everything is made new! All this is from God.

2 CORINTHIANS 5:17-18 NCV

The day is done, the sun has set,
Yet light still tints the sky;
My heart stands still
In reverence,
For God is passing by.

RUTH ALLA WAGER

Girliness is next to Godliness

Something deep in all of us yearns for God's beauty,
and we can find it no matter where we are.
Sue Monk Kidd

Girliness is next to Godliness

The Grand Essentials

Prayer is essential.... Pray hard and long. Pray for your brothers and sisters. Keep your eyes open. Keep each other's spirits up so that no one falls behind.

EPHESIANS 6:13 THE MESSAGE

This is the true joy of life, the being used up for a purpose recognized by yourself as a mighty one; being a force of nature instead of a feverish, selfish little clot of ailments and grievances, complaining that the world will not devote itself to making you happy. I am of the opinion that my life belongs to the community, and as long as I live, it is my privilege to do for it what I can.

GEORGE BERNARD SHAW.

Only a life lived for others is a life worthwhile.

ALBERT EINSTEIN

Girliness is next to Godliness

The grand essentials of happiness are: something to do,
something to love, and something to hope for.
ALLAN K. CHALMERS

_____

_____

_____

_____

_____

_____

_____

_____

_____

_____

Simple Things

Blue skies with white clouds on summer days. A myriad of stars on clear moonlit nights. Tulips and roses and violets and dandelions and daisies. Bluebirds and laughter and sunshine and Easter. See how He loves us!

ALICE CHAPIN

God hasn't invited us into a disorderly, unkempt life but into something holy and beautiful—as beautiful on the inside as the outside.

1 THESSALONIANS 4:7 THE MESSAGE

It's simple things, like a glowing sunset, the sound of a running stream or the fresh smell in a meadow that cause us to pause and marvel at the wonder of life, to contemplate its meaning and significance. Who can hold an autumn leaf in their hand, or sift the warm white sand on the beach, and not wonder at the Creator of it all?

Girliness is next to Godliness

Joys come from simple and natural things: mists over meadows,
sunlight on leaves, the path of the moon over water.
SIGURD F. OLSON

Imagine All You Can

Imagination is the beginning of creation. You imagine what you desire, you will what you imagine and at last you create what you will.

GEORGE BERNARD SHAW

Look up to the skies.
Who created all these stars?
He leads out the army of heaven one by one
    and calls all the stars by name.
Because He is strong and powerful,
    not one of them is missing....
Surely you know. Surely you have heard.
The Lord is the God who lives forever,
    who created all the world.
He does not become tired or need to rest.
No one can understand how great His wisdom is.
He gives strength to those who are tired
    and more power to those who are weak.

ISAIAH 40: 26, 28-29 NCV

Reality can be beaten with enough imagination.

Girliness is next to Godliness

Every person's life is a fairy tale written by God's fingers.
HANS CHRISTIAN ANDERSEN

_____

_____

_____

_____

_____

_____

_____

_____

_____

_____

Cultivate a Spirit of Joy

Joy is the feeling of grinning on the inside.

MELBA COLGROVE

How necessary it is to cultivate a spirit of joy. It is a psychological truth that the physical acts of reverence and devotion make one feel devout. The courteous gesture increases one's respect for others. To act lovingly is to begin to feel loving, and certainly to act joyfully brings joy to others which in turn makes one feel joyful. I believe we are called to the duty of delight.

DOROTHY DAY

Serve each other with love. The whole law is made complete in this one command: "Love your neighbor as you love yourself."

GALATIANS 5:13-14 NCV

Since you get more joy out of giving joy to others, you should put a good deal of thought into the happiness that you are able to give.

ELEANOR ROOSEVELT

Girliness is next to Godliness

A joy that's shared is a joy made double.
ENGLISH PROVERB

It's Such an Interesting World

When I look at the galaxies on a clear night—when I look at the incredible brilliance of creation, and think that this is what God is like, then instead of feeling intimidated and diminished by it, I am enlarged—I rejoice that I am part of it.

MADELEINE L'ENGLE

He counts the number of the stars;
He gives names to all of them.
Great is our Lord and abundant in strength;
His understanding is infinite.

PSALM 147:4-5 NASB

Girliness is next to Godliness

Isn't it splendid to think of all the things there are to find out about? It just makes me feel glad to be alive—it's such an interesting world. It wouldn't be half so interesting if we knew all about everything.
LUCY MAUD MONTGOMERY

_____

_____

_____

_____

_____

_____

_____

_____

_____

Bloom Where You Are Planted

One of the most tragic things I know about human nature is that all of us tend to put off living. We are all dreaming of some magical rose garden over the horizon—instead of enjoying the roses that are blooming outside our windows today.

DALE CARNEGIE

So then neither he who plants is anything, nor he who waters, but God who gives the increase. Now he who plants and he who waters are one, and each one will receive his own reward according to his own labor. For we are God's fellow workers.

1 CORINTHIANS 3:7-9 NKJV

Girliness is next to Godliness

How strange is the lot of us mortals! Each of us is here for a brief sojourn; for what purpose he knows not, though he senses it. But without deeper reflection one knows from daily life that one exists for other people.

ALBERT EINSTEIN

_____

_____

_____

_____

_____

_____

_____

_____

_____

_____

The Rhythm of My Spirit

The time is coming when the true worshipers will worship the Father in spirit and truth, and that time is here already. You see, the Father too is actively seeking such people to worship Him. God is spirit, and those who worship Him must worship in spirit and truth.

JOHN 4:23-24 NCV

Teach me, Father, how to go
Softly as the grasses grow;
Hush my soul to meet the shock
Of the wild world as a rock;
But my spirit, propt with power,
Make as simple as a flower.
Let the dry heart fill its cup,
Like a poppy looking up;
Let life lightly wear her crown,
Like a poppy looking down,
When its heart is filled with dew,
And its life begins anew.

EDWIN MARKHAM

Girliness is next to Godliness

God knows the rhythm of my spirit and knows
my heart thoughts. He is as close as breathing.

_____

_____

_____

_____

_____

_____

_____

_____

_____

_____

Living Life

Fear less, hope more;
Whine less, breathe more;
Talk less, say more;
Hate less, love more;
And all good things are yours.

SWEDISH PROVERB

You have begun to live the new life, in which you are being made
new and are becoming like the One who made you. This new life
brings you the true knowledge of God.

COLOSSIANS 3:10 NCV

Life is about not knowing, having to change, taking the moment
and making the best of it, without knowing what's going to happen
next. Delicious ambiguity.

GILDA RADNER

Girliness is next to Godliness

*The best and most beautiful things in the world cannot
be seen or even touched. They must be felt with the heart.*
HELEN KELLER

_____

_____

_____

_____

_____

_____

_____

_____

_____

The Beautiful Character of a Woman

The most consummately beautiful thing in the universe is the rightly fashioned life of a good person.

GEORGE HERBERT PALMER

Virtue shows quite as well in rags and patches as she does in purple and fine linen.

CHARLES DICKENS

You know me inside and out...You know exactly how I was made, bit by bit, how I was sculpted from nothing into something. Like an open book, You watched me grow from conception to birth; all the stages of my life were spread out before You...before I'd even lived one day.

PSALM 139:15-16 THE MESSAGE

Beauty without virtue is a flower without perfume.

FRENCH PROVERB

Girliness is next to Godliness

She who would have beautiful roses in her garden
must have beautiful roses in her heart.
S. REYNOLDS HOLE

_____

_____

_____

_____

_____

_____

_____

_____

_____

_____

Today and Always

Some say "tomorrow" never comes,
A saying oft thought right;
But if tomorrow never came,
No end were of "tonight."
The fact is this, time flies so fast,
That e'er we've time to say
"Tomorrow's come," presto! behold!
"Tomorrow" proves "Today."

Even though on the outside it often looks like things are falling
apart on us, on the inside, where God is making new life, not a day
goes by without His unfolding grace. These hard times are small
potatoes compared to the coming good times, the lavish celebration
prepared for us. There's far more here than meets the eye. The
things we see now are here today, gone tomorrow. But the things we
can't see now will last forever.

2 CORINTHIANS 4:16-18 THE MESSAGE

Girliness is next to Godliness

Light tomorrow with today.
ELIZABETH BARRETT BROWNING

Beautiful Things

Christ's love makes the church whole. His words evoke her beauty.
Everything He does and says is designed to bring the best out of
her, dressing her in dazzling white silk, radiant with holiness.

EPHESIANS 5:25 THE MESSAGE

Real strength never impairs beauty or harmony, but it often
bestows it; and in everything imposingly beautiful, strength has
much to do with the magic.

HERMAN MELVILLE

We are all cups, constantly and quietly being filled. The trick is,
knowing how to tip ourselves over and let the beautiful stuff out.

RAY BRADBURY

Girliness is next to Godliness

*Though we travel the world over to find the beautiful,
we must carry it with us or we find it not.*
RALPH WALDO EMERSON

_____

_____

_____

_____

_____

_____

_____

_____

_____

The Accessory of Laughter

Humor is perhaps a sense of intellectual perspective: an awareness that some things are really important, others not; and that the two kinds are most oddly jumbled in everyday affairs.

CHRISTOPHER MORLEY

The more you find out about the world, the more opportunities there are to laugh at it.

BILL NYE

A cheerful heart is good medicine.

PROVERBS 17:22 NIV

A well-developed sense of humor is the pole that adds balance to your step as you walk the tightrope of life.

WILLIAM ARTHUR WARD

Girliness is next to Godliness

Good humor is one of the best articles of dress one can wear in society.
WILLIAM MAKEPEACE THACKERAY

_____

_____

_____

_____

_____

_____

_____

_____

_____

_____

The Ultimate Goal

Tell me not, in mournful numbers,
Life is but an empty dream!
For the soul is dead that slumbers,
and things are not what they seem.
Life is real! Life is earnest!
And the grave is not its goal;
Dust thou art; to dust returnest,
Was not spoken of the soul.

HENRY WADSWORTH LONGFELLOW

The goal of our instruction is love from a pure heart and a good conscience and a sincere faith.

1 TIMOTHY 1:5 NASB

Girliness is next to Godliness

The great use of life is to spend it for something that will outlast it.
WILLIAM JAMES

_____

_____

_____

_____

_____

_____

_____

_____

_____

_____

The Need for Nonsense

I like nonsense—it wakes up the brain cells. Fantasy is a necessary ingredient in living. Its a way of looking at life through the wrong end of a telescope...and that enables you to laugh at all of life's realities.

THEODOR SEUSS GEISEL (DR. SEUSS)

"What makes you think the whole world revolves around you?!" my mother said, as I slowly rotated to maintain eye contact.

JOHN ALEJANDRO KING

The Lord is kind and does what is right;
our God is merciful.
The Lord watches over the foolish;
when I was helpless, He saved me.
I said to myself, "Relax,
because the Lord takes care of you."

PSALM 116:5-7 NCV

Girliness is next to Godliness

*Aerodynamically, the bumble bee shouldn't be able to fly, but
the bumble bee doesn't know it so it goes on flying anyway.*
MARY KAY ASH

_____

_____

_____

_____

_____

_____

_____

_____

_____

_____

Let the Day Suffice

The simplest and commonest truth seems new and wonderful when we experience it the first time in our own life.

MARIE VON EBNER-ESCHENBACH

People who don't know God and the way He works fuss over these things, but you know both God and how He works. Steep your life in God-reality, God-initiative, God-provisions. Don't worry about missing out. You'll find all your everyday human concerns will be met.

MATTHEW 6:32-33 THE MESSAGE

Sooner or later we all discover that the important moments in life are not the advertised ones, not the birthdays, the graduations, the weddings, not the great goals achieved. The real milestones are less prepossessing. They come to the door of memory.

SUSAN B. ANTHONY

Girliness is next to Godliness

Let the day suffice, with all its joys and failings, its little triumphs and defeats. I'd happily, if sleepily, welcome evening as a time of rest, and let it slip away, losing nothing.

KATHLEEN NORRIS

_____

_____

_____

_____

_____

_____

_____

_____

_____

Girliness is next to Godliness

Work-a-day World

Attempt easy tasks as if they were difficult, and difficult as if they were easy; in the one case that confidence may not fall asleep, in the other that it may not be dismayed.

BALTASAR GRACIAN

Don't just do what you have to do to get by, but work heartily, as Christ's servants doing what God wants you to do. And work with a smile on your face, always keeping in mind that no matter who happens to be giving the orders, you're really serving God. Good work will get you good pay from the Master.

EPHESIANS 6:6-8 THE MESSAGE

Respect human talent, respond to genius, recognize reality, admire truth and beauty, realize the meaning of the rare flower Reason.

PETER NIVIO ZARLENGA

Girliness is next to Godliness

The secret of joy in work is contained in one word—excellence.
To know how to do something well is to enjoy it.
PEARL BUCK

_____

_____

_____

_____

_____

_____

_____

_____

_____

_____

God's Fingertips

The God who flung from His fingertips this universe filled with galaxies and stars, penguins and puffins...peaches and pears, and a world full of children made in His own image, is the God who loves with magnificent monotony.

BRENNAN MANNING

God is the sunshine that warms us, the rain that melts the frost and waters the young plants. The presence of God is a climate of strong and bracing love, always there.

JOAN ARNOLD

God promises to love me all day, sing songs all through the night! My life is God's prayer.

PSALM 42:8 THE MESSAGE

Girliness is next to Godliness

God's fingers can touch nothing but to mold it into loveliness.
GEORGE MACDONALD

_____

_____

_____

_____

_____

_____

_____

_____

_____

_____

Deep and Powerful Sense

Hope is a state of mind, not of the world. Hope, in this deep and powerful sense, is not the same as joy that things are going well, or willingness to invest in enterprises that are obviously heading for success, but rather an ability to work for something because it is good.

VÁCLAV HAVEL

Hope, like the gleaming taper's light,
Adorns and cheers our way;
And still, as darker grows the night,
Emits a brighter ray.

OLIVER GOLDSMITH

I pray also that the eyes of your heart may be enlightened in order that you may know the hope to which He has called you, the riches of His glorious inheritance in the saints, and His incomparably great power for us who believe. That power is like the working of His mighty strength.

EPHESIANS 1:18-19 NIV

Girliness is next to Godliness

For I am bound with fleshly bands,
Joy, beauty, lie beyond my scope;
I strain my heart, I stretch my hands,
And catch at hope.
CHRISTINA ROSSETTI

_____

_____

_____

_____

_____

_____

_____

_____

The Tapestry of Our Lives

Some people weave burlap into the fabric of our lives, and some weave gold thread. Both contribute to make the whole picture beautiful and unique.

No eye has seen,
no ear has heard,
no mind has conceived
what God has prepared
for those who love Him.

1 CORINTHIANS 2:9 NIV

For whatever life holds for you...in the coming days, weave the unfailing fabric of God's Word through your heard and mind. It will hold strong, even if the rest of life unravels.

GIGI GRAHAM TCHIVIDJIAN

Girliness is next to Godliness

It's the little things that make up the richest part of the tapestry of our lives.

Dear God...

You are a child of your heavenly Father. Confide in Him. Your faith in His love and power can never be bold enough.

BASILEA SCHLINK

We must take our troubles to the Lord, but we must do more than that; we must leave them there.

HANNAH WHITALL SMITH

Embrace this God-life. Really embrace it, and nothing will be too much for you.... That's why I urge you to pray for absolutely everything, ranging from small to large. Include everything as you embrace this God-life, and you'll get God's everything.

MARK 11:22-24 THE MESSAGE

You pay God a compliment by asking great things of Him

TERESA OF AVILA

Girliness is next to Godliness

*Where are you? Start there. Openly and freely
declare your need to the One who cares deeply.*
CHARLES SWINDOLL

_____

_____

_____

_____

_____

_____

_____

_____

_____

_____

_____

Walking with God

Just as a prism of glass miters light and casts a colored braid, a garden sings sweet incantations the human heart strains to hear. Hiding in every flower, in every leaf, in every twig and bough, are reflections of the God who once walked with us in Eden.

TONIA TRIEBWASSER

All the way to heaven is heaven begun to the Christian who walks near enough to God to hear the secrets He has to impart.

E. M. BOUNDS

If we walk in the light as He is in the light, we have fellowship with one another, and the blood of Jesus Christ His Son cleanses us from all sin.

1 JOHN 1:6-7 NKJV

God walks with us.... He scoops us up in His arms or simply sits with us in silent strength until we cannot avoid the awesome recognition that yes, even now, He is here.

GLORIA GAITHER

Girliness is next to Godliness

Whoever walks toward God one step, God runs toward him two.
JEWISH PROVERB

_____

_____

_____

_____

_____

_____

_____

_____

_____